Bruce Springsteen
The Illustrated Biography

Bruce Springsteen
The Illustrated Biography

CHRIS RUSHBY

Trans
Atlantic
Press

For Alison

Published by Transatlantic Press
First published in 2010

Transatlantic Press
38 Copthorne Road
Croxley Green
Hertfordshire
WD3 4AQ

© Transatlantic Press
Photographs © Getty Images

ISBN 978 – 907176 – 15 – 9

Printed and bound in China

Contents

Introduction

From a troubled childhood in suburban New Jersey, Bruce Springsteen has made a unique musical journey to become one of the world's most popular and enduring stars. As a writer, singer, guitarist, recording artist, and performer he has formed an emotional bond with his audience of a strength few other entertainers have ever managed.

Bruce Frederick Joseph Springsteen was born on September 23, 1949, the only son of Adele and Douglas Springsteen. He has two sisters, Virginia and Pamela. His childhood was a difficult one, there being seemingly nothing much that inspired the young Springsteen other than "the power and the majesty and the ministry of rock 'n' roll," as he later put it. Although he remained unconverted and skeptical, the effects of Springsteen's Catholic education on his world view also show through in the lyrics of many later songs and the old-time religious feel of moments in the live shows. His New Jersey upbringing was also to color Springsteen's later career; he returned with his family to live there and is engaged with the local community in ways most people with his degree of fame and fortune would long ago have ceased to contemplate.

There was very little the young Springsteen wanted to do but make music. He was inspired by seeing and hearing Elvis Presley to buy his first guitar and begin to learn his craft. His mother saved the money to buy the 16-year-old Bruce a better model, typical of her efforts to nurture his career. The relationship with his father is also pivotal to the way the boy developed, more because of a lack of sympathy than its presence. Springsteen later said, only partly tongue in cheek, of his relationship with his father: "what would I conceivably have written about without him? I mean, you can imagine that if everything had gone great between us, we would have had disaster. I would have written just happy songs ..."

He has done much more than that. Shrugging off the "new Bob Dylan" tag, Springsteen achieved worldwide fame with Born to Run. His concerts, both alone and with the E Street Band, are legendary for his stage presence, charisma, and energy. After the "Bruce-mania" years of Born in the USA came the so called lost decade of the 90s, as Springsteen broke up the band and experimented with his music, not wholly successfully. An E Street reunion in 1999 signaled the beginning of a return to form. The Rising was a heartfelt response to 9/11. The tour that followed, along with the subsequent strong albums and hundreds of live shows that followed over the past few years, have cemented Springsteen's reputation as one of the great songwriters and performers of our time.

Chapter One

The E Street Shuffle

Growin' up

Opposite and right: The loner with a guitar from the back streets of New Jersey found at least some sense of community in rock music. In early bands the Castiles and Earth, Springsteen began to learn his trade in small local venues. Another of Springsteen's early bands, Steel Mill, featured Dan Federici, Vini Lopez, and, eventually, Steve Van Zandt, all to be part of what eventually became the E Street Band, the band that has remained with Springsteen, largely unchanged in its membership, to this day. Also, for the first time he began to write and sing his own material and it was also around this time that Springsteen began to be known as "The Boss" by his bandmates, a soubriquet this natural rebel and outsider has long struggled to come to terms with.

Working his craft

Opposite and right: Springsteen, a slightly more relaxed and bohemian looking figure than in earlier years. In the early 1970s Springsteen was continuing to work at his craft, looking for the right sound and the elusive big break. Bands with names like the Sundance Blues Band, the Bruce Springsteen Band and even Dr. Zoom & the Sonic Boom were all vehicles showcasing Bruce's talent that didn't quite do the trick.

Springsteen's song-writing, as much as his live performances, was what eventually brought him to the brink of fame. He first acquired a new manager, the hustling Mike Appel. Appel's efforts got Springsteen noticed by John Hammond, the legendary CBS producer, promoter, and discoverer of stars such as Bob Dylan, Billie Holiday, and Benny Goodman among others. Prodded by Appel, Hammond eventually auditioned Springsteen in 1972 and it was at this point the young artist's career began to move.

The "new Dylan"

Opposite: Springsteen sports
a leather jacket to match
his girlfriend's hair. When
Hammond signed Springsteen,
he brought to the studio with
him several of the musicians
who would go on to form the
E Street Band. Springsteen's
first album, *Greetings from
Asbury Park, NJ*, was released in
January 1973 and immediately
established him as a critical
success, if not immediately a
commercial one.

Right: The songs on *Greetings*
... and the quickly established
persona of rebel rock 'n' roller
with a songwriting gift (along
with the presence in his career
of Dylan's early mentor, John
Hammond) soon earned
Springsteen the unwanted tag of
"the new Dylan." He could have
done without this millstone,
expectations engendered by it
having blighted the careers of
more than one promising young
singer-songwriter before him.

Releasing a second album

Above and opposite: Springsteen with then current girlfriend, Karen Darvin (who went on to marry musician Todd Rundgren). In September 1973 Springsteen released his second album, *The Wild, the Innocent and the E Street Shuffle*. The music once again gained critical acclaim, but commercial success still eluded Bruce.

Springsteen's songs seemed to be becoming ever grander gestures and the lyrics of epics like "Rosalita" and "4th of July Asbury Park (Sandy)" are still firm favorites with fans and concert audiences. Both Springsteen and his record company were disappointed and frustrated by the lack of a commercial breakthrough. This was eventually to come in 1975, though, with a career- and life-transforming third album.

The future of rock 'n' roll

Left: Springsteen on the Born to Run tour. In May 1974 the rock critic John Landau saw Springsteen live in concert and wrote afterwards: "I saw rock and roll future, and its name is Bruce Springsteen. And on a night when I needed to feel young, he made me feel like I was hearing music for the very first time." Landau was to become both Springsteen's manager and producer and would work with him on the later sessions for the legendary *Born to Run* album.

Opposite: The Born to Run tour hits the Bottom Line club in New York. Columbia gave Springsteen one more chance to make a big hit record. In spite of the big budget allotted to the project, Springsteen found himself bogged down in the recording process, trying to find a way to get the sounds in his head onto vinyl. The album eventually took around 14 months to complete, and expectation among fans was high.

Born to Run

Right: The Boss and the Big Man: Bruce on stage with saxophonist Clarence "Big Man" Clemons, one of the stalwarts of the E Street Band. Clemons' and Springsteen's images in iconic silhouette feature on the *Born to Run* album cover. It was during these long drawn out album sessions that Steve Van Zandt (who had already featured in earlier Springsteen musical projects) drifted back into his life and into the band; and it was Van Zandt who helped nail some of the intractable *Born to Run* material.

Tasting success

Opposite: Clarence and Bruce
at the Bottom Line, where
Springsteen and the E Street
Band played a five night residency
in August 1975, just ahead
of the long awaited album's
release. *Rolling Stone* magazine
names this ten concert run
as one of its "50 Moments
That Changed Rock and Roll."
Media commentators attended
these shows in droves and the
E Streeters gave consistently
brilliant performances of old
and new material. Springsteen's
huge energy and charisma on
stage, already apparent to a niche
audience, seemed suddenly public
knowledge.

Right: Springsteen on stage at the
Electric Ballroom on the Born to
Run tour. *Born to Run* was finally
released on August 25, 1975, and
at last Springsteen began to taste
the success that had eluded him.
The record climbed the charts,
an instant and huge success with
Springsteen's existing fans, but
also bringing him a new fan base,
attracted to the huge sweep of
sound and imagery in the new
album. Songs like "Born to Run,"
"Thunder Road," "Jungleland,"
and "Tenth Avenue Freeze-Out"
are all major Springsteen tracks
and still provide highlights of
live shows.

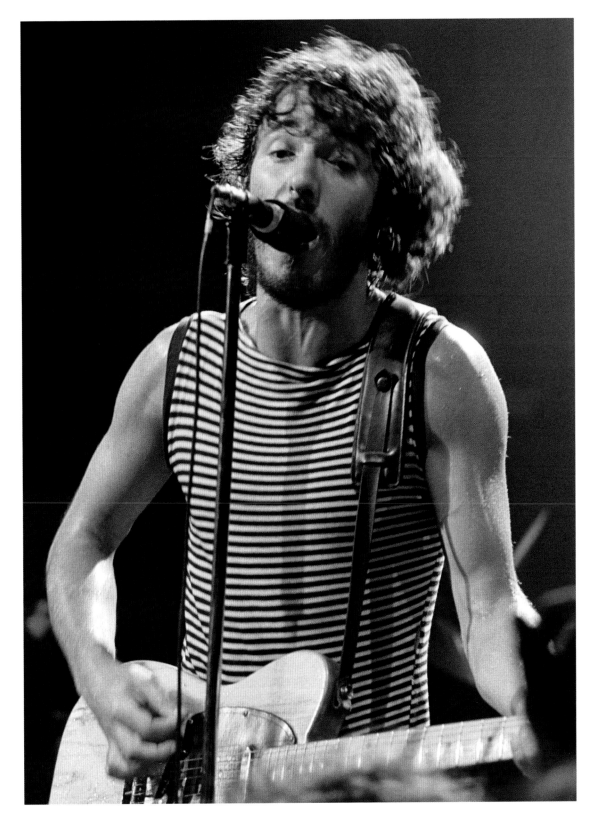

Glory days

Opposite and right: Bruce on stage at the Electric Ballroom. *Born to Run* is considered by many to be one of the best rock albums of all time. It definitively established Springsteen as a major artist, with its Spectoresque wall of sound, its panoramic imagery, and the singer's hard-won humor and optimism in the face of a dark, dirty world. Springsteen was—and still is—seen as a blue collar hero, speaking for and mythologizing the American working man

Springsteen was a cultural phenomenon, appearing in the same week of October 1975 on the covers of both *Time* and *Newsweek* magazines. He had all the fame he could handle and the concerts in support of the bestselling album continued to win him fans in the US and beyond.

Wilderness years

Left: Just when success beckoned, in a strange twist of fate Springsteen became involved in a protracted legal dispute with his former manager, Mike Appel. For around two years the dispute and its attendant court case effectively prevented Springsteen from going into the studio to record new material, a frustrating situation to say the least for an artist brimming with creative ideas and the desire to capitalize on *Born to Run*'s success.

Opposite: Springsteen on stage with an unusually dapper Steve Van Zandt. Bruce and the band stayed together while the court case rumbled on, touring across the US with their high energy shows. Meantime, Springsteen was writing and beginning to perform darker material than that featured on his previous album.

E Street magic

Opposite: Springsteen on the piano (literally), with keyboardist Dan Federici and Clarence Clemons of the E Street Band. Along with Roy Bittan, a second keyboard player, and with Max Weinberg on drums, Garry Tallent on bass, and Van Zandt on guitar, the nucleus was there for a tight-knit lineup that has endured largely unchanged for three decades or more.

Above: The bearded Springsteen of the mid-70s acknowledges the applause. Bruce and the band honed their craft in these difficult years. Had they not toured hard, it's possible the band would have split apart during the recording hiatus, and it is to Springsteen's credit that he kept the show on the road during these dark days.

The darkness lifts

Above: Bruce on stage with Southside Johnny (of Southside Johnny and the Asbury Dukes fame) at the Stone Pony club, Asbury Park. Southside and Springsteen both came from the New Jersey scene and Bruce has never deserted his roots, making frequent appearances in Jersey venues and continuing to perform with those he mixed with in the early days.

Opposite: A nonchalant-looking Springsteen during a radio interview. When a legal settlement was finally reached with Mike Appel in 1977, Springsteen was finally able to return to the recording studio. What came out of these new recording sessions was a sound quite different from the ebullience of *Born to Run*: the new disk, *Darkness on the Edge of Town*, was altogether darker, leaner, and more reflective. Its author appeared to be thinking harder about life and politics than had previously been the case in his writing.

Darkness on the Edge of Town

Above: Springsteen and Van Zandt in the recording studio in 1978 during the sessions that produced *Darkness on the Edge of Town*. Although not one of his bestselling records, many core Springsteen fans consider this one of his strongest. Tracks such as "Badlands" and "The Promised Land" still feature in concerts.

Opposite: Bruce in the midst of his audience in Bloomington, Minnesota, 1978. The concerts that promoted *Darkness* ... were massive and awe inspiring displays by the band, even by their already high standards. Springsteen has always connected physically with his audiences and as recently as 2009 was seen stage-diving into the crowd, trusting to the loyalty and muscle of fans to catch his fall and transport him safely back to the stage.

"I asked myself new questions...."

Right: Springsteen on stage in 1978. The band were playing
four hour sets, mixing exuberant material from the earlier
days with the darker, more introspective themes of *Darkness*.
Springsteen was audibly growing up and grappling with
more serious issues, without the concerts ever losing their
extroversion, spirit, and sense of fun and rock 'n' roll. "I
had a reaction to my own good fortune. I asked myself new
questions ... I had to infuse the music with my own hopes and
fears," said Springsteen of the writing of the new album.

"Well I got this guitar...

Opposite: ... and I learned how to make it talk." Springsteen and Telecaster on stage at the Forum in July 1978. Those unfamiliar with the live act were occasionally confounded by what sounded like booing from fans; it would invariably turn out to be the affectionate cries of "Broooce" from a audience intent on calling their hero's name between songs.

Above: On stage at the Fox Theater, Atlanta, Georgia, September 1978. The 118-date Darkness tour finally ended in January 1979, by which time Springsteen's reputation was at an all-time high with both critics and American public. The power and passion of his music, then as now, marked him out as a unique talent.

A hungry heart

Opposite and right: Springsteen with then girlfriend, the photographer Lynn Goldsmith, in February 1979. The relationship was to end later that year. In April 1979 singer and band were back in the studio once more to begin recording tracks for the album that was to become the massively successful *The River*.

The River was a grand, sprawling double album showing Springsteen still developing as a songwriter. Not finally released until the following year, the singer found the recording process and final selection of material from his prolific output of songs a particularly difficult one.

No Nukes

Opposite: Taking time out from recording *The River*, Springsteen performs at one of the No Nukes benefit concerts at Madison Square Garden, New York, on September 21, 1979. Organized by MUSE (Musicians United for Safe Energy) to raise awareness of issues around nuclear energy production, Springsteen was persuaded to participate by his friend Jackson Browne.

Right: A beatific Bruce dances with an audience member. *The River* was released in October 1980, to yet more acclaim. Upbeat, crowd pleasing rockers like "Ramrod" and "Hungry Heart," Springsteen's first top ten hit single, mix with more somber, self-searching material like "Independence Day" (tackling the troubled relationship with his father) and "Wreck on the Highway."

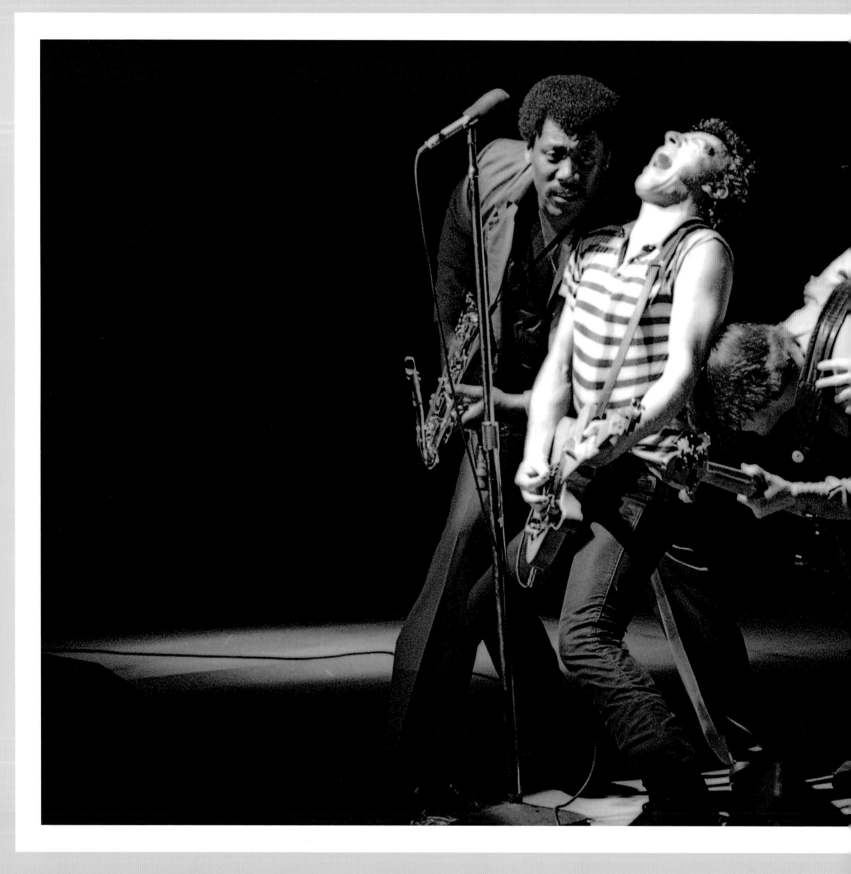

Touring The River

Left: The E Street Band in London 1981 with Clemons, Springsteen, Tallent, and Van Zandt on stage at Wembley Arena. *The River* sold massively and the tour that followed it was a long one, including an extended run of concerts in Europe. Very apparent in these shows (and at almost every Springsteen show before and since) is the amazing extent of the artist–audience empathy, something few other performers have ever come close to achieving on the scale Springsteen manages it.

Nebraska

Above: Springsteen on the deck, with Garry Tallent behind. Following *The River*, Springsteen's music took a quite different turn with the dark, acoustic songs of *Nebraska*. The material had originally been intended to be played with the E Street Band. Having tried unsuccessfully to record some of them that way, Springsteen and Jon Landau eventually decided that the solo acoustic demos Springsteen had recorded, in his home studio on a four-track tape deck, represented the sound that most suited these stark, depressed ballads.

Opposite: Clarence and Steve lend Bruce their support in 1981. The *Nebraska* sessions produced several songs that did not find their way onto the album, but sounded better with the E Street sound; these began to form the basis for Springsteen's next, and in many ways, most awesome album of all ...

Reasons to believe

Opposite: Springsteen with Clarence Clemons. While *Nebraska* did not sell as well as many of his albums, it enhanced the artist's credibility and won him much critical praise. The spare, pared-down "lo-fi" sound and the dark honesty of the music went on to influence many other artists and albums.

Springsteen chose not to tour with the dark, quiet songs from *Nebraska*.

Above: June 1982 and Springsteen shares a New York stage with Jackson Browne at another anti-nuclear benefit concert.

Born in the USA

Opposite: Springsteen on stage on the massive worldwide tour to support the *Born in the USA* album. This is one of the bestselling albums of all time and no less than seven singles taken from it entered the American top ten, including the title track,"I'm on Fire," and "Dancing in the Dark." The tour was a massive success and found Springsteen yet more new adherents beyond his already large and diverse fan base.

Above: Springsteen and Patti Scialfa on stage. Scialfa joined the E Street band as a backing singer in time for the tour. At around this time Steve Van Zandt made the decision to leave to pursue his own musical goals. He was replaced on guitar by Nils Lofgren, a hugely talented player who fitted quickly into the E Street lineup.

Dancing in the Dark

Above: Springsteen dancing with Courtney Cox for the video of "Dancing in the Dark." This was the biggest hit of all the *Born in the USA* songs, helped by an eye-catching video directed by Brian de Palma and recorded early in the tour. The video also helped kick-start the career of the then unknown *Friends* actress, plucked from the audience to dance with Springsteen at the end of the song. In quite different but equally high profile appearances in 1985, Springsteen was also to feature on the "We Are the World" charity record.

Opposite: Springsteen on stage in July 1984 on the Born in the USA tour.

Tour 1984–5

Opposite: Bruce shows those muscles. Bodybuilding gave Springsteen a beefed-up look he had never previously displayed—and perhaps encouraged some of the sleeveless shirts favored on the tour. The term "Bruce-mania" was coined around this time, as the tour wound on around the world, with Springsteen causing a stir wherever the band pitched up.

Above: Patti Scialfa supporting Springsteen in July 1984.

The Big Man

Right: Clarence "Big Man" Clemons and Springsteen on stage in 1984. The highest profile of all the E Streeters and perhaps the best loved by fans, Clemons is the last to be introduced by his boss to the audience at the end of concerts ("the man who's known all around the world as ... the king of the world") and gets the biggest audience cheer of any band member.

Record-breaking tour

Left: Springsteen on stage in October 1984 during the Born in the USA tour.

Right: A year later, playing the last show of the Born in the USA tour on October 2, 1985 at the Los Angeles Memorial Coliseum. The end of the tour marked Springsteen's highest ever point of public visibility and the tour and album gave him the broadest audience he'd ever have. A new album, *Live 1975–85*, released in 1986, documents Springsteen and the E Street band in some of their best moments up to that point. It's easy to hear the effect Springsteen has on audiences and understand the power he has to get 100,000 people singing along with just a wave of his hand.

Rockin' All Over the World

Above: Bruce and Patti on stage at the Oakland Coliseum arena.

Opposite: Springsteen takes a guitar solo. The tour had been Springsteen's longest and most successful to date, grossing around $90 million and selling out massive stadia around the world. The band had played to tens of thousands of fans at each of the 156 shows.

The world's greatest live act

Right: Nils Lofgren, Clarence Clemons, and Springsteen on stage on the Born in the USA tour. All this mid-80s popularity spawned a number of Springsteen fanzines, the most notable of which, *Backstreets,* continues today, both as a glossy publication and online, providing fans with up-to-the-minute news to a level and with a speed only dreamed of in previous decades.

Julianne

Opposite and right: Julianne
Phillips and Bruce Springsteen.
Phillips was the youngest
of six children and from a
middle class background that
contrasted markedly with
Springsteen's and was the
singer's junior by eleven years.
As a successful young model
she was dubbed "the perfect ten
package." Although best known
as Bruce's first wife, Phillips
had a number of high profile
acting roles including that of
Frankie Reed in the American
TV drama *Sisters*. Phillips and
Springsteen met during the
Born In The USA tour and were
soon married, in Lake Oswego,
Oregon, on May 13, 1985, after
a whirlwind courtship. Both the
ceremony itself and the couple's
relationship were the subject
of intense media interest. The
marriage, however, was not
to last.

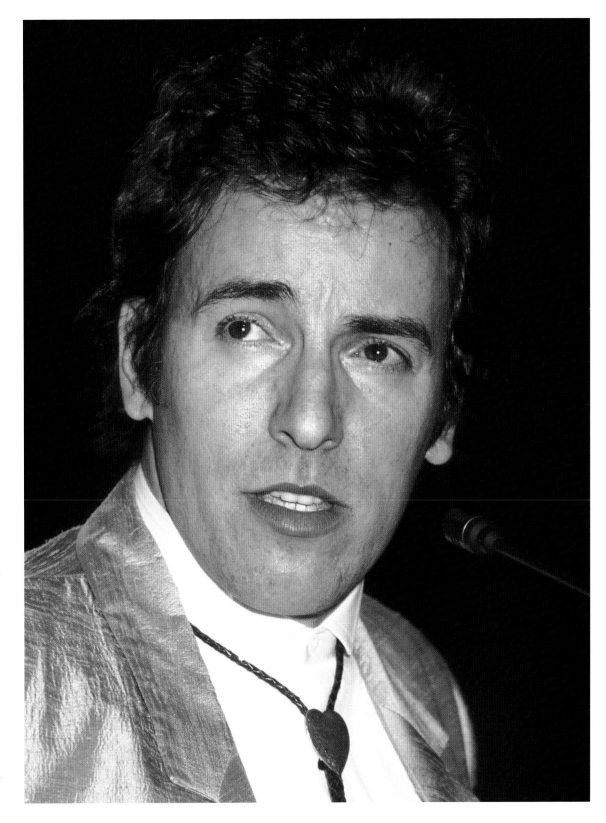

Rock and Roll Hall of Fame

Opposite and right: In January 1987 Springsteen appeared at the Rock and Roll Hall of Fame dinner to induct Roy Orbison. The clean cut, glitzy figure he cut at the award ceremony was some distance from the scruffy bohemian look of the Born in the USA concerts. Springsteen was to become a regular attendee at Rock and Roll Hall of Fame events and was himself inducted in 1999.

The Big "O"

Opposite Roy Orbison is inducted into the Rock and Roll Hall of Fame by Springsteen.

Above: Roy Orbison celebrates his Hall of Fame induction in the after dinner concert, joined by Bo Diddley, Smokey Robinson, Springsteen, and others. Springsteen had long been a fan of the older artist, who went on to find renewed fame late in his life as one of the Traveling Wilburys, a supergroup including George Harrison and Bob Dylan among other luminaries.

Tunnel of Love

Left: Springsteen was by now working on songs that would eventually be released on the *Tunnel of Love* album. This was to be a quieter and more reflective album than its predecessor, though it once again spawned a number of hit singles and sold well.

Opposite: Springsteen performs at Harry Chapin's World Hunger Forum benefit concert at Carnegie Hall, New York, in 1987. Chapin, who died young, had lobbied Springsteen hard to support his charity work. Springsteen did so and has continued to carry out charitable work over the years, sometimes quietly and other times very publicly.

Miami Steve

Left: Springsteen and "Miami" Steve Van Zandt. Possibly Springsteen's closest friend, Van Zandt has had a varied career beyond the E Street Band, including his role in the *Sopranos* TV series and as DJ on his popular radio show.

Opposite: Springsteen on stage with harmonica in 1988. Apart from the brilliance of his guitar work, Springsteen's wailing harmonica is almost as much a musical trademark of his as it is of Bob Dylan's. He also occasionally plays piano and bass.

Chapter Two

Tunnel of Love

More Rock and Roll Fame

Opposite: Jeff Lynne (of ELO and Traveling Wilburys fame), Mick Jagger, and Springsteen at the Rock and Roll Hall of Fame induction evening, January 1988.

Above: George Harrison, Springsteen, and Mick Jagger perform together at the 1988 Rock and Roll Hall of Fame induction concert. Springsteen is one of the world's greatest live acts and rehearses hard for his own shows. On the other hand he always seems ready to take to the stage for impromptu sets and simply have a good time with fellow performers.

Ain't Got You

Above: Bruce and Julianne look happy, but during the European leg of the tour rumors were flying and it eventually became public knowledge that Springsteen was linked romantically with E Street backing singer Patti Scialfa. Phillips and Springsteen filed for divorce in 1988, with the divorce being finalized the following year.

Opposite: On stage during the Tunnel of Love Express tour.

Tunnel of Love Express Tour

Opposite: The 1987 album *Tunnel of Love* seemed to describe unhappiness in a relationship, although he denied the songs were about trouble in his own marriage. Springsteen and the band went out on tour with the new songs in 1988, on what was billed the Tunnel of Love Express tour. There were different arrangements of old songs, a horn section, and some fans were slightly troubled at Springsteen's temerity in rearranging his own material. In spite of such grumbles, the shows were once again well received.

Right: Bruce ready for a night on the town.

A new relationship

Left: Springsteen with Patti Scialfa in 1988 at the time their relationship became public. Like her future husband, Scialfa was born and brought up in New Jersey. Before and during her time with Springsteen and E Street, music has been a major part of Scialfa's life: she gained a music degree from New York University and has released three successful solo albums, not to mention appearances on numerous others as a backing singer.

Opposite: September 1, 1988: at the press conference for the Amnesty Human Rights Now! tour, Peter Gabriel, Springsteen, Sting, and Tracy Chapman pose for the cameras.

Amnesty tour

Left: The Human Rights Now! tour was a worldwide journey by the artists involved, raising funds and awareness on behalf of Amnesty International. Springsteen and the E Street Band were joined on the tour by Peter Gabriel, Sting, Tracy Chapman, and Youssou N'Dour for a memorable series of concerts that did a great job of publicizing the causes Amnesty espoused, visiting countries and venues not often reached by Western rock acts.

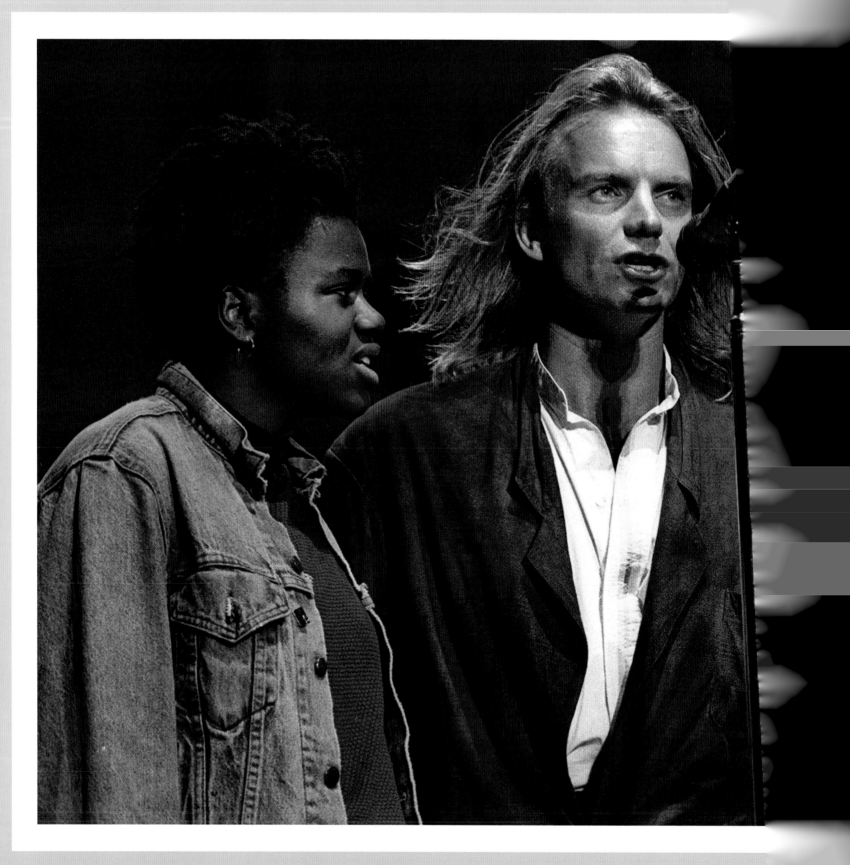

Crowd pleasers

Left: Tracy Chapman, Sting, and Springsteen at the JFK Stadium in Philadelphia, Pennsylvania, in September 1988 on the Amnesty Human Rights Now! tour. The E Street Band would generally close the show with a set of crowd pleasing greatest hits, before the whole cast came back back for collaborations and encores.

Chimes of Freedom

Opposite: A serious Springsteen on stage. The Amnesty tour breached the Iron Curtain when it reached Hungary. When it reached the Third World, most of the shows were played free to local audiences.

Right: Bruce and Patti arrive at an awards ceremony. By this time Scialfa was of course Springsteen's partner as well as being a regular member of the E Street Band, but it was not long after this that Springsteen delivered a shock to their other bandmates.

End of E Street

Opposite: In January 1989 it was announced that the E Street Band would no longer work together. Springsteen had phoned the other members individually to tell them that he wanted to move on and that they should feel free to pursue other musical directions. It was a huge shock to most of the band, as well as to its many fans. Springsteen, though, was going through various kinds of personal turmoil and had decided that, musically, he needed to try doing things differently in future.

Above: Springsteen performing on stage in New York with Paul Simon in January 1989.

Family man

Opposite: Bruce and Diana Ross on stage in January 1990. Although the E Street Band was apparently no more, relations between Springsteen and his former band members were generally still cordial. Keyboard player "Professor" Roy Bittan played Springsteen some music he had been working on and the two began to collaborate on tracks that would, it was soon determined, feature on the next Springsteen album.

Above: Bruce and Patti at a dinner in 1990. Their son, Evan, was born in this year.

Music after E Street

Opposite: Springsteen performs with rhythm and blues singer Lavern Baker in 1991. The music Springsteen and Bittan had cowritten was destined for what was to become Springsteen's next album, *Human Touch*, which was finally nearing completion. But *Human Touch* was not the only album to be released by Springsteen when the mixing was finally completed in 1992.

Above: Springsteen takes the stage with Phoebe Snow, Chaka Khan, Bonnie Raitt, and others at a 1991 Rock and Roll Hall of Fame event. In parallel with the *Human Touch* music, Springsteen came up with a set of songs somewhat different in character. After much deliberation, it was decided to issue both *Human Touch* and a second, slightly folksier album, *Lucky Town,* simultaneously and let the fans decide between them—or, hopefully, buy both.

Human Touch tour

Opposite: Springsteen in July 1992 as the Human Touch tour hits London's Wembley Arena. *The Human Touch* and *Lucky Town* albums had been recorded with session musicians, Bittan and Scialfa providing the only links with the E Street Band.

Right: In Chicago, August 1992, on the *Human Touch* tour. Springsteen's world tour to promote his new music was strange for some attendees, in that an almost completely different group of musicians backed him (not the E Street Band and not even the same lineup as the players who had accompanied him on these two albums), to the disappointment and consternation of some diehard E Street fans.

A talented pair

Above: Springsteen performing live with guitarist and song writer John Fogerty (of Creedence Clearwater Revival fame) at a Rock and Roll Hall of Fame induction ceremony in May 1993. Springsteen was later to duet with Fogerty on one of the latter's albums.

Opposite: May 1993: Springsteen with his battered but trusty Telecaster on the UK leg of the Human Touch tour, at the Milton Keynes Bowl, where a typically high energy performance converted any doubters among the crowd.

Plugged

Opposite: Springsteen at Milton Keynes. Springsteen had recorded a performance in November 1992 for
the MTV *Unplugged* series, although after the first song his performance became defiantly "plugged," with
his live band joining him on stage for a rousing evening. Released in 1993 as a CD and video, the songs and
arrangements prepared those attending the 1993 shows for the kind of band and sounds they would hear.

Above: January 1994 and Springsteen performs with the Guns N' Roses star Axl Rose.

Oscar winner

Opposite: Springsteen has
won many awards in his
time, including a number of
Grammys. In 1994 he also won
an Academy Award for his song
"Streets of Philadelphia," part
of the soundtrack of Jonathan
Demme's powerful and
sensitive movie *Philadelphia*.
The video for the song
apparently shows Springsteen's
actual vocal performance,
recorded with a hidden
microphone, as he walks the
streets of the city.

Right: Springsteen with Whitney
Houston at the Oscars.
Springsteen grasps his "Streets
of Philadelphia" award.

Famous friends

Above: The annual Elton John AIDS Foundation party at the 1994 Academy Awards. Oscar winner Bruce and Patti share a table with Elton, Steven Spielberg, and Tom Hanks, star of *Philadelphia*.

Opposite: Springsteen in shades, black leather, and bling. In spite of successes such as the Oscar, the 90s were not his best times: "I didn't do a lot of work. Some people would say I didn't do my best work," Springsteen was subsequently quoted as saying.

Blood Brothers

Left: Bruce dressed for the street. The multimillionaire rarely looks other than the man-of-the-people rock and roller he remains at heart. In 1995 there was a brief reunion of the E Street Band: new songs were recorded for a *Greatest Hits* album and a documentary, *Blood Brothers*, was made of the recording sessions for those tracks.

Opposite: Shopping on the streets of New York, Springsteen wanders, apparently unrecognized, down Madison Avenue. Having found such huge fame Springsteen manages, better than almost any other star of comparable celebrity, to stay level headed and in touch with reality, never seeming to turn his back on his roots.

Ghost of Tom Joad

Opposite: 1995 brought another musical change of direction, when Springsteen released *The Ghost of Tom Joad*. The music was spare, the melodies often lacking, and the album featured mostly just Springsteen on guitar. The songs were direct and political, championing the cause of the immigrant and underdog, inspired by a Pulitzer Prize winning book, *Journey to Nowhere*. Although similar to *Nebraska* in some ways, this was one of Springsteen's least popular albums, although once again earning him credibility as a voice for the dispossessed. Springsteen toured the world with *The Ghost of Tom Joad* songs, without any band in tow.

The somber, austere figure on the stage still attracted big audiences and treated them to radical rearrangements of some of his earlier songs in the style of the *Tom Joad* material. Springsteen often demanded silent attention to what he was performing from fans who just wanted to sing along as they were used to doing at Bruce's shows.

Above: Springsteen and Clarence Clemons at the Grand Opening of the Rock and Roll Hall of Fame, Cleveland.

Back to New Jersey

Left: Bruce and Patti stepping out at the MTV Music Awards. Following the Ghost of Tom Joad tour, Springsteen, who had been living on the west coast, moved back with his family to his beloved New Jersey, where they have remained.

Opposite: Bruce with troubled producer Phil Spector. Though they never worked together in the studio, Spector's famous dense, layered "wall of sound" production technique was the inspiration for the sound of the breakthrough *Born to Run* album, and so Spector could be said to be partly responsible for Springsteen's success.

Activist

Left: Springsteen at the Rainforest Foundation benefit concert in 1995. Springsteen has become more politically aware and active over the years and has felt increasingly able to speak his mind and stand up for causes he believes in.

Opposite: In October 1996 Springsteen with the Reverend Jessie Jackson at a concert opposing "Prop 209." In the contentious debate, Springsteen lent his weight to the campaign pressing for affirmative state action to support racial, sexual, and ethnic minorities.

More famous friends

Left: Bruce with singer and guitarist Bonnie Raitt at Rhythm and Blues Foundation's Pioneer Awards. The talented Raitt was one of the foundation's trustees.

Opposite: With Jakob Dylan at a Radio City concert rehearsal for the 1997 MTV Music Awards ceremony, where Springsteen joined the younger Dylan's band, the Wallflowers, for a performance. Jakob Dylan's famous father was, along with Elvis Presley, one of the greatest musical influences on Springsteen's music and, particularly, on his writing.

In court

Left: In October 1998 Springsteen looks unusually smart for a court appearance in London. There, he successfully sued a UK company for publishing pirate recordings of some of his very early material. On learning that his case had been won Springsteen was quoted as saying, "I am very happy. I was not here for the money but for my music."

Opposite: At a benefit concert for slain policeman Sergeant Patrick King in 1998. This was the year in which Springsteen released a sprawling four-disk set of outtakes called *Tracks*. It had long been clear that Springsteen tended to write far more material than actually appeared on albums, and *Tracks* collected many of the unreleased gems. The material excited loyal fans, but this was as nothing compared to the news that 1999 was to mark the reunion of the E Street Band...

E Street reunion

Opposite: In the UK, May 1999, on the E Street reunion tour. Springsteen had finally got the need to plow his own furrow out of his system; he came once again to value the camaraderie of his friends and the quality of the music they all made together. Everyone was a little older, but the magic was still very much there.

Above: On stage with Van Zandt at Earls Court, London, on the UK leg of the reunion tour. The tour lasted over a year and broke box office records around the world. The band has toured extensively in the years since and, although Springsteen has involved himself in other projects from time to time, he has made it clear he believes the band are playing better than ever and that he will keep on working with them as long as they can keep going.

Inducted into the Hall of Fame

Opposite: Three of the best guitarists in the business: Lofgren, Springsteen, and Van Zandt in the Netherlands on the 1999 reunion tour. This was the first time the band regularly featured both Van Zandt and Lofgren (who had replaced Van Zandt as principal guitarist) together in the lineup. The tour finally ended with ten sold-out nights at New York's Madison Square Garden. A recording of the band in concert taken from the last two nights at the Garden was subsequently released as the CD and video Bruce Springsteen and the *E Street Band: Live in New York City.*

Above: He had been a regular attendee at these ceremonies and inducted others, but in March 1999 Springsteen, seen with Clarence Clemons and Steve Van Zandt, was himself inducted into the Rock and Roll Hall of Fame in a ceremony in New York. U2's Bono presented Springsteen with the award.

Little Steven and The Boss

Opposite: In November 2001, at the Spotlight Awards benefit gala and auction in New York, Springsteen presents Steve Van Zandt with the Spotlight Award.

Above: Springsteen appears to be settling in to read a very long speech about Van Zandt at the Spotlight Awards. Throughout his long career Springsteen has been generous to a fault in acknowledging his musical debts to others, presenting awards, guesting on albums, and helping to push the careers of unknown artists.

Remembering an activist

Opposite: Springsteen performs "Thunder Road" at the Leonard P. Zakim Bunker Hill Bridge dedication ceremony, watched by Zakim's widow. Zakim was a Jewish-American civil rights campaigner who died in 1999. The high profile Zakim never managed to fulfill one particular star-spotting ambition: "I've had my picture taken with the Pope, Bruce Springsteen, and the Dalai Lama. Now I've got to get the three of them together."

Left: Bruce and Patti in July 2001. The Springsteen marriage has been an untypically successful rock and roll union, producing three children and with the Springsteens still together after more than twenty years.

9/11 and The Rising

Opposite: The events of September 11, 2001, had a profound effect on America and there is a well known story that, a few days later, Springsteen was parking his car in the Jersey Shore town of Sea Bright when a fan drove by. The man rolled down his window, shouted, "We need you!" and drove on. If Springsteen had not already been galvanized by the dreadful events, this moment apparently made him see his responsibilities.

The Rising, released in July 2002, was Springsteen's first full studio album with the E Street Band for 18 years. This powerful music reflects, sometimes obliquely and sometimes directly, on the 9/11 attacks. It was both a critical and popular success.

Left: Bruce and Patti at a Nordoff-Robbins charity dinner at the beginning of 2002.

Chapter Three

The Rising

The Rising Tour

Right: Nils Lofgren and Springsteen looking happy and relaxed on stage in Amsterdam during The Rising tour, October 2002. *The Rising* became Springsteen's bestselling new album for 15 years and, once again, the band embarked on a world tour of arena shows to promote it, the longstanding lineup being augmented by Soozie Tyrell on violin.

Waitin' on a Sunny Day

Above: Bruce and Patti at a rehearsal for the launch of the new album. Altogether, The Rising tour took in 82 cities and the band played 120 shows over the course of 14 months on the road, beginning on August 7, 2002 at the Continental Airlines Arena, New Jersey.

Opposite: Performing with Clarence Clemons on the Rising tour, December 2002. The tour once again marked some unprecedented events, including ten sold-out concerts at the Giants Stadium. The tour concluded in October 2003 with three nights at Shea Stadium, during the last of which Bob Dylan took the stage as a guest to sing with Springsteen.

The Ministry of Rock and Roll

Above: The E Street Band in action: Clemons, Tallent, Springsteen, Van Zandt, and Scialfa rock the crowd in Las Vegas. Springsteen is quoted as saying, "I believe that the life of a rock and roll band will last as long as you look down into the audience and can see yourself, and your audience looks up at you and can see themselves—and as long as those reflections are human, realistic ones."

Opposite: The E Street Band play at the MTV Video Music Awards.

Bruce and Elvis

Left: Springsteen and Elvis Costello rehearse
for a performance at the 45th Grammy
Awards ceremony, where *The Rising*
won the Grammy for Best Rock Album.
Springsteen and Costello have appeared on
stage together a number of times, including
an appearance by Springsteen on Costello's
Spectacle TV talk show.

London Calling

Above: No Doubt bassist Tony Kanal, Springsteen, and Dave Grohl of the Foo Fighters share a joke backstage at the rehearsal for the Grammys in February 2003.

Opposite: Dave Grohl, Tony Kanal, Pete Thomas on drums, and Springsteen perform the song "London Calling" at the Grammy Awards as a tribute to the late Joe Strummer of the Clash. Costello was also in this all-star lineup. Springsteen has since performed the song live a number of times, while on tour with the E Street Band.

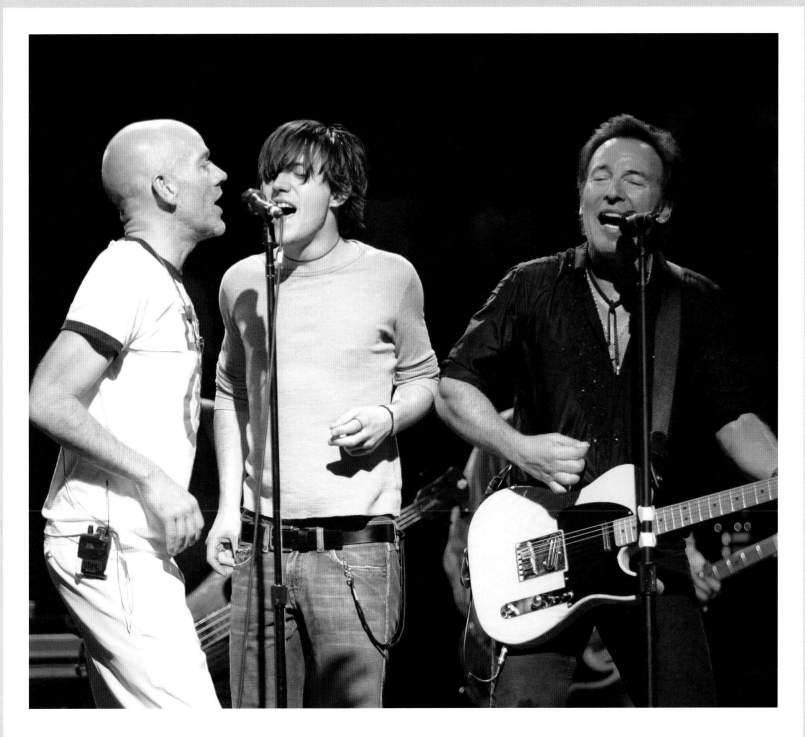

Vote for Change

Opposite: A tired but happy-looking Bruce. In 2004 Springsteen and the band joined the Vote for Change tour, along with Pearl Jam, REM, Jackson Browne, and numerous other musicians. The concerts aimed to encourage people to register and vote and were held in swing states.

Above: REM's Michael Stipe, Conor Oberst of Bright Eyes, and Springsteen play at a Vote for Change concert in October 2004 in Philadelphia.

Barcelona

Left: Bruce and Patti on stage in Barcelona on The Rising tour. The city seems to contain some of Springsteen's most loyal and extrovert fans, concerts there being among the most memorable he plays in terms of audience participation. A DVD entitled *Bruce Springsteen and the E Street Band: Live in Barcelona* provided a visual record of the tour.

Opposite: Wisconsin Governor Jim Doyle introduces Springsteen on stage at a campaign concert.

This Land Is Your Land

Left: Bruce on the campaign trail. Springsteen has become engaged more closely with mainstream liberal politics. When *Born in the USA* came out, Springsteen demanded that Ronald Reagan cease quoting the title song of his album in campaign speeches. He did not, however, go as far as formally endorsing Reagan's opponent, Walter Mondale. His support for John Kerry and more recently for Barack Obama has been more overt.

No Surrender

Opposite: October 2004, and Springsteen performs in Columbus, Ohio, to support Senator John Kerry's presidential campaign. Previously Springsteen had refused any explicit endorsement of political candidates, but this time he decided to take a stance, earning himself praise in some quarters while alienating others.

Above: Springsteen and John Kerry together acknowledge the crowd. Springsteen's *Born in the USA* song "No Surrender" became the theme song for Kerry's (ultimately unsuccessful) campaign, and Springsteen would perform acoustic versions of it at Kerry rallies.

Devils & Dust

Above: Springsteen with Senator John Kerry and his wife Teresa. A new solo Springsteen album was released in April 2005. *Devils & Dust* was another low key album along the lines of *Nebraska* and *The Ghost of Tom Joad*, although with slightly more instrumentation than those albums.

Opposite: Some of the *Devils & Dust* songs had in fact been written around the time of the Ghost of Tom Joad tour, performed then, but never released. As with most of his solo acoustic work, the new album received a relatively muted public response.

Let's Rock It

Left: Springsteen in conversation with former astronaut and veteran US Senator John Glenn. The title track of *Devils & Dust* is about the feelings of a soldier in Iraq. Springsteen undertook a solo tour to support the album, although album sales were relatively modest and audience figures were, by his standards, slightly disappointing in some venues, perhaps reflecting the "difficult" nature of some of the material.

Opposite: Springsteen performs live for the VH1 *Storytellers* TV series. On the Devils & Dust tour Springsteen ventured well beyond acoustic guitar, performing on piano, pump organ, ukelele, banjo, and a number of other instruments.

Bring 'em home

Left: At the Bercy Stadium in Paris on the
European leg of the Devils & Dust tour
in June 2005. At the Grammy Awards
broadcast, where he was nominated for
several awards for the album, Springsteen
gave the audience a passionate rendition of
the song "Devils & Dust," adding the line
"Bring 'em home" at the end of the song
and then leaving the stage without waiting
for the applause.

Playing with Bono

Opposite: Springsteen with
Bono in March 2005 at the Rock
and Roll Hall of Fame Awards,
at which U2 were inducted.

Right: Bruce and Patti on the
town with Trudie Styler and
husband Sting in New York,
2005. Springsteen had become
friends with his fellow Amnesty
tour star and the two have met
regularly over the years.

Anniversaries and tributes

Left: In November 2005 a 30th anniversary edition of the *Born to Run* album was released, making some Springsteen fans feel suddenly quite old.

Opposite: Springsteen sings at the MusiCares James Taylor concert. In 2006, singer James Taylor was awarded the MusiCares Person of the Year Award. At a filmed concert in Taylor's honor a host of celebrities including Paul Simon, Jackson Browne, David Crosby, and the Dixie Chicks joined Springsteen to perform songs from Taylor's repertoire. Springsteen gave a masterly rendition of Taylor's song "Millworker."

Redheaded women

Opposite : A thoughtful Springsteen backstage at the James Taylor concert. The 30th anniversary reissue of *Born to Run* was accompanied by a video of a legendary performance from November 1975 by Springsteen and the band at the Hammersmith Odeon in London. The full CD of this concert was released a little later and marked the first ever Springsteen concert to be captured in full on CD.

Above: Between two redheaded women: Bonnie Raitt and Patti Scialfa pose with Springsteen at the James Taylor evening.

A tribute from a friend

Opposite: Springsteen with his old friend Sting. Years later, at the concert celebrating Springsteen being given a Kennedy Center award, Sting was to deliver a hugely powerful performance of Springsteen's song "The Rising," causing the whole audience, including President and Mrs. Obama, to get to their feet and sway to the music. Sting once said of his friend, "The great thing about Bruce is that he's exactly as he seems: a great man."

Above: Springsteen with the actress Maria Bello at the James Taylor MusiCares evening.

We Shall Overcome

Opposite: At a performance rehearsal for the 48th Grammy Awards evening in 2006, Springsteen and Elvis Costello discuss the finer points of the show they are about to give. In April 2006 Springsteen released a new album, *We Shall Overcome: The Seeger Sessions*. This represented something of a change of direction for the singer: from the E Street Band, only Scialfa and Soozie Tyrell joined Springsteen in a crew of 18 folk and roots musicians playing mostly traditional music.

Above: Sam Moore (the soul singer, of Sam and Dave fame), Springsteen, and Elvis Costello at the 48th Grammy Awards. The Seeger Sessions music was inspired by and celebrated Pete Seeger's brand of musical activism and his folk credentials. The album was recorded in just three days of loose, informal sessions.

Grammys 2006

Opposite: Paul McCartney and Springsteen pose together for a photograph at the 2006 Grammys. The Beatles' triumphant invasion of the United States inspired a generation of youngsters and influenced the young Bruce's musical education. "Twist and Shout" was apparently the first song Springsteen learned.

Above: Springsteen, Elvis Costello, and others perform a New Orleans Tribute at the 48th Grammy Awards evening, following the devastation to the city caused by Hurricane Katrina. Springsteen took the Seeger Sessions music on the road in what was advertised as "an all-new evening of gospel, folk, and blues."

New Orleans in the spotlight

Above: U2's The Edge and Springsteen at the Grammys' New Orleans tribute.

Opposite: Bruce in the spotlight. There was both an American and two European legs of the Seeger Sessions tour. A CD and film taken from November 2006 were released the following June: *Bruce Springsteen with the Sessions Band: Live in Dublin* was a fine memento of these warm hearted shows An early success for the Seeger Sessions tour came at the New Orleans Jazz & Heritage Festival on April 30, 2006. Springsteen criticized government handling of the Katrina disaster, to the loud approval of the audience.

Soul men

Opposite: Springsteen and Sam Moore on stage. Springsteen duetted with Moore on one of the latter's albums and Moore returned the compliment, featuring on several songs on Springsteen's *Human Touch* in 1992.

Right: Springsteen on harmonica and acoustic guitar. His 15th studio album, entitled *Magic,* was released in 2007. This marked a return to recording with the E Street Band, although one of the songs, "Long Walk Home," had been written some time previously and performed with the Seeger Sessions band. A "hidden" track on the album was "Terry's Song," a tribute to Springsteen's friend and assistant Terry Magovern, who died in July 2007, shortly before the album was finished.

Magic

Right: Mr. and Mrs. Springsteen out shopping. There was great anticipation among fans for the first E Street Band record in five years. The first single from the *Magic* album was "Radio Nowhere," which became a number 1 hit record in numerous territories.

Opposite: Bruce and Patti at Jan Wenner's 60th birthday party. Wenner, the editor of *Rolling Stone* magazine, has interviewed Springsteen several times and *Rolling Stone* has featured him on its cover on numerous occasions.

The Magic tour

Opposite: The Springsteen and E Street Band tour to support the *Magic* album began almost simultaneously with its release and rolled on through north America and Europe into 2008.

Above: Sister Soozie Tyrell and Springsteen on stage. The Magic tour marked a sad moment in the long history of E Street Band friendships: keyboard player Danny Federici, a friend of Springsteen's for longer than any other member, had to leave the tour in November 2007 to pursue treatment for melanoma. Federici was to return in March 2008 for one last, emotional performance with the band, but sadly succumbed to the disease and died in April 2008. Springsteen said, "Danny and I worked together for 40 years—he was the most wonderfully fluid keyboard player and a pure natural musician. I loved him very much ... we grew up together."

On the road

Opposite: The E Street Band hits Houston, Texas, in April 2008, on the Magic tour. Springsteen said of his late bandmate Federici, "Of course we all grow up and we know 'it's only rock and roll' ... but it's not. After a lifetime of watching a man perform his miracle for you, night after night, it feels an awful lot like love." His bandmates—and his audience, too—would probably say that of Springsteen himself.

Above: Clarence Clemons performs with Springsteen in San Jose, California, on the Magic tour. Clemons too has suffered health problems in recent years, having knee joint replacements, undergoing back surgery, and even suffering a mild heart attack. Although not as mobile as in earlier years he is, however, determined to continue as part of the band as long as the band itself continues.

Giants Stadium

Left: July 2008, and Springsteen communes with the crowd at the Giants Stadium, Meadowlands, New Jersey. This was almost a home fixture for the E Streeters and they played the stadium often over the years. In 2009 Springsteen and the band would give the final show ever performed at Meadowlands, before its scheduled demolition and replacement with a new stadium. A new Springsteen song, "Wrecking Ball," was an affectionate tribute to the venue and its imminent demise.

Two Hearts Are Better Than One

Opposite: Miami Steve Van Zandt and Springsteen on stage at the Giants Stadium. After Federici's death the remaining band members have, unsurprisingly, been more conscious of mortality and the fact the band can't go on forever. Springsteen and Van Zandt continue to relish both friendship and onstage camaraderie after several decades on the road together.

Above: In July 2008 daughter Jessica and son Evan Springsteen appear together with their parents on stage at the Nou Camp Stadium, Barcelona, Spain. Jessica is an equestrian star and competes at national level. Evan, although studying at college, has dipped a toe in the water of rock and roll and has joined his father and the band on stage to play guitar.

Piano man

Right: Springsteen makes a rare appearance
at the piano. With two keyboard players
already in the band in the shape of Roy
Bittan and Dan Federici (latterly replaced
in the lineup by Charles Giordano from
the Seeger Sessions band), it's not often
Springsteen ventures to the keyboards
himself.

Playing with Grin

Opposite: Nils Lofgren and Springsteen on stage at Cardiff Millennium Stadium in June 2008. A hugely talented musician, Lofgren has recorded with numerous other artists, including Neil Young, and has released well regarded albums of his own when not working with Springsteen. Although thought of as the new boy in the band, he has worked with Springsteen for over a quarter of a century.

Above: Springsteen back stage displaying his favored approach to beard growing of the past few years. In April 2008 Springsteen had announced publicly his support of Senator Barack Obama in his bid for the US presidency.

Supporting Obama

Opposite: Sam Springsteen, Bruce's son, meets Barack Obama on the campaign trail. In endorsing Obama's campaign, Springsteen spoke of the importance of "truth, transparency, and integrity in government, the right of every American to have a job, a living wage, to be educated in a decent school, and a life filled with the dignity of work, the promise and the sanctity of home."

Above: Springsteen and Senator Obama share the stage. Springsteen made a number of solo acoustic performances in support of Obama. One of these featured a new song called "Working on a Dream," performed in a duet with Patti Scialfa, that seemed entirely appropriate to the mood of optimism abroad in the campaign.

The Dream

Opposite: Springsteen performs for Obama and tens of thousands of supporters in Cleveland, Ohio, in November 2008. "The Rising" was a fitting and moving inclusion and brought some of the crowd to tears.

Above: Bruce and Patti with Barack and Michelle Obama at the Cleveland rally. In thanking Springsteen for his support, Obama said, "There are just a handful of people who enter into your lives through their music and tell the American people's story; Bruce Springsteen is one of those people."

Back to Philadelphia

Left: October 4, 2008, and Springsteen joins the Obama election campaign on one of what were billed as the Vote for Change concerts. His seven song acoustic set included Woody Guthrie's "This Land Is Your Land," and Springsteen himself cut a Guthrie-esque figure on stage.

Opposite: Springsteen sings for Obama in Philadelphia in front of 50,000 people. These were emotional performances, with Springsteen urging the crowd to vote for Obama and change America's political direction.

Behind the shades

Left: Springsteen on a sunny day on the Obama campaign trail. Following President Obama's election victory speech in front of 240,000 people, one of the pieces of music played was Springsteen's song "The Rising." The new song "Working on a Dream" was not the only one Springsteen had been working on. He had continued to write new material after finishing *Magic* and the band would record during breaks on the tour. All the songs were written quickly, Springsteen said, and often recorded in the first few takes in the studio.

Golden Globe

Opposite: Springsteen with actor Mickey Rourke at the Golden Globe Awards party in January 2009. Springsteen won the Golden Globe for Best Song for "The Wrestler." He had written the song, at Rourke's request, for the latter's new film, the story of a washed-up fighter that was to revitalize Rourke's career, the success of the film helped in no small part by Springsteen's powerful and affecting song.

Right: Springsteen poses with Darren Aronofsky, director of *The Wrestler.*

At the Lincoln Memorial

Opposite: Springsteen opened the musical proceedings at We Are One: the Obama Inaugural Celebration on January 18, 2009. Held at the Lincoln Memorial in Washington, the event was attended by over 400,000 people. Springsteen again performed "The Rising," this time with a large choir.

Above: Springsteen with Pete Seeger at the Obama inaugural concert, performing "This Land Is Your Land." Seeger, an influence not just on Springsteen but on several generations of musicians, had obviously inspired the Seeger Sessions music.

Inaugural concert

Opposite: Springsteen performs on a cold Washington day at the Obama inaugural concert. The *Working on a Dream* album was released in January 2009 and marked another stage in what was coming to seem like one of Springsteen's most sustained periods of creativity. His 24th album, it earned positive reviews, topped the charts in a number of countries, and prompted yet another tour by the band, in what seemed like a simple refusal to contemplate resting after the Magic jaunt.

Above: Springsteen with singer Beyoncé at the Obama inaugural concert in Washington DC.

Appearing at the Super Bowl

Opposite: Springsteen does his famous "whirling the guitar around the body" move at the Super Bowl concert, while Van Zandt and Scialfa are content simply to play theirs. Springsteen and the E Street Band (not to mention a large choir) performed at the prestigious half-time show at the Super Bowl on February 1, 2009, to thousands in the stadium and millions of live TV viewers from around the world.

Above: Bruce and Patti at the press conference for the Super Bowl show. Springsteen promised fans a "12 minute party" and that's exactly what the band delivered, in a tightly choreographed, high energy, crowd pleasing set, including "Tenth Avenue Freeze-Out," "Born to Run," "Glory Days," and "Working on a Dream."

Glory Days

Left: Springsteen rocks the Super Bowl. Asked about the pressure of playing live in front of such a huge audience, Springsteen replied, "You'll have a lot of crazy football fans, but you won't have Lincoln staring over your shoulder. That takes some of the pressure off," in an allusion to his recent appearance in Washington at the Obama inaugural concert.

Opposite: Van Zandt, Scialfa, and Springsteen at the Super Bowl concert. Springsteen acknowledged that this had probably been the busiest month of his professional life; for a man in his 60th year The Boss shows no signs of slowing down.

Happy Birthday, Pete Seeger

Left: Joan Baez, Springsteen, Pete Seeger, and Patti Scialfa at Seeger's 90th birthday celebration concert. Known as the Clearwater Benefit Concert and held in New York's Madison Square Garden, the event attracted a host of artists including Emmylou Harris, Billy Bragg, Dave Matthews, and Kate & Anna McGarrigle.

Opposite: Arlo Guthrie and Springsteen perform at the Clearwater concert for Pete Seeger's birthday in May 2009. Guthrie's father, Woody, was a big influence on Bruce, who has often performed the Guthrie anthem "This Land Is Your Land."

The Working on a Dream Tour

Opposite: Springsteen in Bilbao, July 2009, during the Working on a Dream tour. This tour set off in April, heading for Europe later in the year. One notable feature of this year's sets was Springsteen's willingness to take song requests from the audience, who would hold up signs indicating their choices. In some of the concerts Max Weinberg, with prior commitments to his role in the house band of Conan O'Brien's *Tonight Show*, was replaced on drums by his son Jay.

Above: Patterson Hood, Billy Bragg, Tom Morello (of Rage Against the Machine), Scialfa, and Springsteen on stage at the Pete Seeger birthday concert.

Living the dream

Left: The E Street Band in full flow. During the Working on a Dream tour, Springsteen and the band (unusually for them) appeared at various summer music festivals, including the Bonnaroo Music Festival in the US and a powerful performance at Glastonbury in the UK. Although some of the new songs were featured, the tour was notable for the number of obscure back-catalog songs dug out of the vaults by Springsteen. During the latter part of the tour the band for the first time also featured performances of whole Springsteen albums such as *Born to Run*, *Darkness on the Edge of Town*, *Born in the USA*, and *The River*, to the delight of fans.

Tomorrow Never Knows

Left: Nils Lofgren, Springsteen, and Soozie Tyrell on stage in the Netherlands, 2009. The Working on a Dream tour ended in November 2009, there being a sense that—while not necessarily the last time the band would be together on the road—this marked something like the end of an era for the E Streeters.

Above: Springsteen and Van Zandt at the Bonnaroo Music & Arts Festival, June 2009.

Kennedy Center Honors Award

Opposite and above: In December 2009 Springsteen was one of the recipients of a Kennedy Center Honors award for his contribution to American culture (pictured here with fellow recipients Robert De Niro, Mel Brooks, Grace Bumbry, and Dave Brubeck along with Secretary of State Hillary Clinton). In presenting Springsteen with the award, Barack Obama remarked, "I'm the President, but he's the Boss." In his seventh decade Springsteen shows no sign of wanting to stop working and millions of fans around the world await whatever new work will next display the humor, passion, and warmth for which he is loved.

KENNEDY CENTER HONOR

DECEMBER 6, 2009

Chronology

1949

September 23: Birth of Bruce Frederick Joseph Springsteen to Douglas and Adele of Freehold, New Jersey.

1958

Discovers rock and roll through seeing Elvis Presley on *The Ed Sullivan Show*.

1963

Buys his first proper guitar from a pawn shop.

1964

Joins his first band, the Rogues, soon moving on to the Castiles.

1966

May 22: With the Castiles, enters a recording studio for the first time and they record songs cowritten by Springsteen (although the songs are never released).

1967

January: The Castiles play the Café Wha in New York's Greenwich Village, their highest profile concerts to date; but the band is not destined to last.

June 19: Graduates high school, later enrolling for a liberal arts course at a nearby college, although he only lasts a year on the course.

1969

The rest of the Springsteen family moves to California. Springsteen plays in more early bands like Earth, Child, and Steel Mill, meeting future E Street Band members Vini "Mad Dog" Lopez and organist Danny Federici.

1970

January: Steel Mill play a number of shows in California, one of which gets a positive review from journalist Philip Elwood, who calls it "one of the most memorable evenings of rock in a long time."

February 22: Steel Mill record three demo songs for legendary promoter Bill Graham, but refuse a recording contract because they think the offered advance is too low.

1971

A year of different bands, including Dr. Zoom & the Sonic Boom (early–mid-1971), the Sundance Blues Band (mid-1971), and the Bruce Springsteen Band (mid-1971–mid-1972).

November: Meets his future manager Mike Appel, who says of the young Springsteen: "There was never any doubt in my mind that he was one of the greatest."

1972

March: Signs a management contract with Mike Appel (later to be the subject of a notorious and protracted lawsuit).

May 2: With Appel, meets the legendary Columbia talent scout John Hammond, who says of

Springsteen, "I knew at once he would last a generation." Further auditions and a demo recording session follow.

June 9: Signs to CBS Records for a $25,000 advance.

November 12: Following his record deal, reunites some of his old bandmates and the newly named E Street Band plays its first show in York, Pennsylvania. The band goes on to record Springsteen's first album, over three weeks of sessions.

1973

January 5: Release of debut album, *Greetings from Asbury Park, NJ*.

June 14: His record company try to boost his profile and Springsteen is the opening act for Chicago at Madison Square Garden, New York. The act is not a success.

November 5: Release of second album, *The Wild, the Innocent* and the *E Street Shuffle*. Like the first album, it is a critical success, but a commercial flop.

1974

April: While on tour with the E Street Band, meets critic and Rolling Stone writer Jon Landau, who is to have a major influence on his career.

May 22: Landau's review is published, with its now famous line "I saw rock and roll's future and its name is Bruce Springsteen."

August: Pianist Roy Bittan and drummer Max Weinberg join the E Street Band, completing the classic lineup.

1975

August 13–17: To rave reviews, Springsteen and the E Street Band play a five night, sold-out series of concerts at the Bottom Line in New York City.

September 1: After many months of frustration in the recording studio, latterly helped by Landau, the *Born to Run* album is released and Springsteen is almost instantly recognized as a star, the title track of the album becoming one of his and rock music's classic songs.

October 27: Springsteen's image features on the covers of both *Time* and *Newsweek* magazines in the same week.

November: In London to play the famous shows at the Hammersmith Odeon.

1976

July 2: Tensions have been increasing between Springsteen and manager Mike Appel, who writes saying he will not allow Jon Landau to produce the next record.

July 27: Sacks Appel as manager; start of the legal wrangle between them that is to drag on for ten months.

1977

May 28: Appel and Springsteen settle, freeing Landau and Springsteen to record together again.

June 1: Recording starts, for what will eventually become *Darkness on the Edge of Town*.

1978

May 23: Start of the biggest E Street Band tour so far, with 118 dates played over seven months.

June 2: After long gestation, release of the Landau-produced *Darkness on the Edge of Town*.

1979

January 1: End of the Darkness tour in Cleveland, Ohio.

March: Begins rehearsing new songs for what will become *The River*.

May: Meets energy activist Tom Campbell and accepts his request to play a benefit concert for MUSE (Musicians United for Safe Energy)

September: Plays MUSE concerts at Madison Square Garden.

1980

October 17: Releases double album *The River*.

October 18: The single "Hungry Heart" is released, providing Springsteen's first top ten hit.

November 5: The night after Ronald Reagan is elected President, Springsteen makes a rare political statement from the stage: "I don't know what you thought about what happened last night," he tells the audience, "but I thought it was pretty terrifying."

1981

May–June: The tour reaches the UK, where Springsteen plays for the first time in more than five years, to huge audience acclaim.

1982

January: Begins recording the songs for *Nebraska*.

September 20: The album *Nebraska* is released. Reviews are good but sales mediocre by Springsteen's recent standards.

1983

Works carefully on the material that is to become the *Born in the USA* album.

1984

May: Guitarist Steve Van Zandt officially leaves the E Street Band. Nils Lofgren replaces him.

June 29: Vocalist Patti Scialfa joins the band.

June 4: Release of *Born in the USA*.

June 8: The massive Born in the USA tour kicks off with a show at the Stone Pony in New Jersey.

October: Meets actress and model Julianne Philips and they begin a whirlwind courtship.

1985

February: Participates in the star-studded recording of "We Are the World," which raises $200 million for victims of the Ethiopian famine as part of the USA for Africa campaign.

February 26: Wins his first Grammy award for Best Male Vocal Performance, for the song "Dancing in the Dark."

May 13: Marries Julianne Philips in Lake Oswego, Oregon.

1986

June 1: Start of the European leg of the Born in the USA tour.

June: Contributes to another star-studded charity musical collaboration, this time Steve Van Zandt's "Sun City" anti-apartheid record.

1986

February: Turns down an offer of $12 million from Chrysler to use "Born in the USA" in an advertising campaign.

November 4: Releases the first ever album box set, the five LPs of *Live 1975–85*.

1987

January: Inducts Roy Orbison into the Rock and Roll Hall of Fame.

October 6: Releases the *Tunnel of Love* album.

1988

February: Start of the Tunnel of Love Express tour with the E Street Band and, for the first time, a horn section.

May: Springsteen and Julianne Phillips separate.

August 30: Julianne Phillips files for divorce.

September–October: The E Street Band headlines the Amnesty International Human Rights Now! tour, featuring Sting, Peter Gabriel, Youssou N'Dour, and Tracy Chapman along with Springsteen.

1989

March 1: The divorce from Julianne Phillips is finalized.

September 23: Springsteen's 40th birthday, celebrated on stage in New Jersey.

October: The E Street Band is "fired" by Springsteen.

1990

July 25: A son, Evan James, is born in Los Angeles.

1991

April: Buys a $14 mansion in Beverly Hills.

June 8: Marries Patti Scialfa at their home in Beverly Hills.

December 30: Birth of daughter Jessica Rae.

1992

March 31: Releases two new albums simultaneously: *Human Touch* and *Lucky Town*. Both receive lukewarm reviews. The subsequent tours to support this new material are undertaken without the E Street Band, to the sadness and disappointment of some fans, although others are happy simply to see The Boss at work.

May 9: Makes his US network television debut on *Saturday Night Live* to promote the new material.

September 22: Records a session for the MTV *Unplugged* series, although plugging in and playing electric with a band after the first song.

1993

Further touring in support of the latest albums.

1994

January 5: Birth of second son, Sam Ryan.

March 21: The song "Streets of Philadelphia" wins an Oscar for Best Original Song.

1995

January 9: Records new material with the E Street Band, to be included in a greatest hits album to be released later in the year.

March 1: "Streets of Philadelphia" wins three Grammys for Song of the Year, Best Male Vocal Performance, and Best Rock Song.

March 18: A *Greatest Hits* album is released, including the new material recorded with the E Street Band.

November 25: Releases *The Ghost of Tom Joad*, in support of which he begins his first solo acoustic tour, lasting 18 months in total.

1997

February 26: *The Ghost of Tom Joad* wins a Grammy for Best Contemporary Folk Album.

May 5: Awarded the Polar Music Prize in Stockholm.

1998

April 26: Death of Springsteen's father, Douglas, from cancer.

November 10: Releases the four-CD album, *Tracks*. This brings rare and unreleased material from the Springsteen vaults.

December 8: A reunion tour with the E Street Band is announced.

December 10: Awarded $500,000 in his successful lawsuit against a UK company releasing some of his early demo tapes.

1999

March: European tour dates announced for Bruce Springsteen and the E Street Band Reunion tour.

March 15: Springsteen is inducted into the Rock and Roll Hall of Fame by Bono.

April 9: Reunion tour starts in Barcelona, Spain.

Mid-July: The tour arrives in the US for a 15-night series of concerts in New Jersey. It continues into 2000.

2000

July 1: The reunion tour ends with a ten-night stand at New York's Madison Square Garden. The last three shows are taped and later released as *Live in New York City*.

2001

April 3: Release of *Live in New York City*.

September 11: Deeply affected by the 9/11 attacks, Springsteen writes new songs ahead of the *America: A Tribute to Heroes* charity TV event, but opts at the last moment to perform "My City of Ruins" instead, a song about the decline of Asbury Park that fits the occasion well.

2002

July 30: Release of *The Rising*, many of the songs on which are influenced by the events of 9/11. The album is a major success, both critical and popular; Springsteen embarks on a major world tour to promote it.

2003

The Rising tour continues for the greater part of the year.

October: Participates in the Vote for Change tour supporting Democratic Senator John Kerry's bid for the presidency.

November: release of *The Essential Bruce Springsteen*, a comprehensive collection of songs that includes a remarkable third disk of unreleased material. This is followed shortly afterwards by *Live in Barcelona*, a DVD memento of the tour just completed.

2005

April: Performs on an episode of the VH1 *Storytellers* TV series, providing revealing insights into the composition of some of his best-known material.

April: Release of a new album, *Devils & Dust*, another low key and somber collection of material.

November: Release of the 30th anniversary edition of *Born to Run*, complete with a new, unseen DVD film of the historic 1975 Hammersmith Odeon show.

2006

February: Wins the Grammy for Best Solo Rock Vocal Performance for Devils & Dust.

April: Releases *We Shall Overcome: The Seeger Sessions*. This is an album of traditional music, with a large backing band led by Springsteen in spirited and often joyful interpretations of traditional songs associated with Pete Seeger.

2007

July 30: Death of Terry Magovern, Springsteen's long-time friend and assistant.

October: Release of the *Magic* album and beginning of a world tour to support the record.

Keyboard player Dan Federici has to leave the tour due to illness.

2008

April 17: Death of Springsteen's friend and bandmate Dan Federici from cancer.

April: Announces his endorsement of Senator Barack Obama for the US presidency.

October: Plays acoustic performances at Obama campaign events.

November 2: Debut of the song "Working on a Dream" at an Obama rally.

November 4: His song "The Rising" is the first music played after Obama's victory speech.

2009

January: Release of the *Working on a Dream* album.

January 11: Wins the Golden Globe award for Best Song for "The Wrestler," written at actor Mickey Rourke's request for his film of the same name.

January 18: Watched by 400,000

people, Springsteen plays the opening music at We Are One: The Obama Inaugural Celebration held at Washington's Lincoln Memorial.

February 1: Performs with the E Street Band at half-time at the Super Bowl.

April 1: First show of the *Working on a Dream* tour in San Jose, California.

May 3: Takes part in the Clearwater Concert at Madison Square Garden, in celebration of Pete Seeger's 90th birthday.

October: Plays at one of the concerts to celebrate the Rock and Roll Hall of Fame's 25th anniversary.

December 6: Among the recipients of the Kennedy Center Honors, presented by President Obama: "While I am the President, he is the Boss," jokes Obama.

2010

January 22: Performs on the *Hope for Haiti* TV fundraising event organized by George Clooney.

Discography

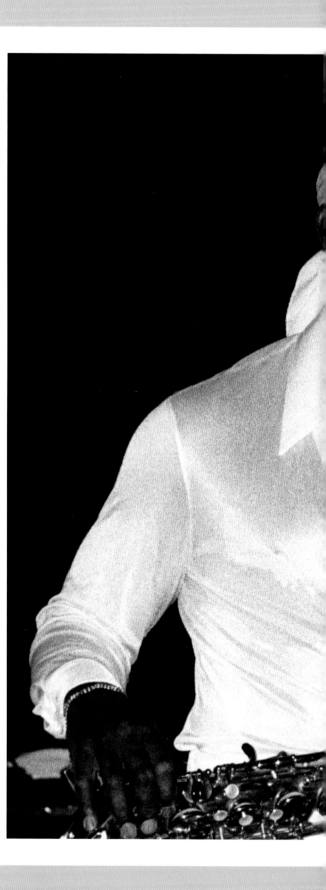

ALBUMS

1973
GREETINGS FROM ASBURY PARK, N.J.

Blinded by the Light
Growin' Up
Mary Queen of Arkansas
Does This Bus Stop At 82nd Street?
Lost in the Flood
The Angel
For You
Spirit in the Night
It's Hard to Be a Saint in the City

1973
THE WILD, THE INNOCENT & THE E STREET SHUFFLE

The E Street Shuffle
4th of July, Asbury Park (Sandy
Kitty's Back
Wild Billy's Circus Story
Incident on 57th Street
Rosalita (Come Out Tonight)
New York City Serenade

1975
BORN TO RUN

Thunder Road
Tenth Avenue Freeze-Out
Night
Backstreets
Born to Run
She's the One
Meeting Across the River
Junglelandw

1978

DARKNESS ON THE EDGE OF TOWN

Badlands
Adam Raised a Cain
Something in the Night
Candy's Room
Racing in the Street
The Promised Land
Factory
Streets of Fire
Prove It All Night
Darkness on the Edge of Town

1980

THE RIVER (DOUBLE ALBUM)

The Ties That Bind
Sherry Darling
Jackson Cage
Two Hearts
Independence Day
Hungry Heart
Out in the Street
Crush on You
You Can Look (But You Better Not Touch)
I Wanna Marry You
The River
Point Blank
Cadillac Ranch
I'm a Rocker
Fade Away
Stolen Car
Ramrod
The Price You Pay
Drive All Night
Wreck on the Highway

1982

NEBRASKA

Nebraska
Atlantic City

Mansion on the Hill
Johnny 99
Highway Patrolman
State Trooper
Used Cars
Open All Night
My Father's House
Reason to Believe

1984

BORN IN THE U.S.A.

Born in the U.S.A.
Cover Me
Darlington County
Working on the Highway
Downbound Train
I'm on Fire
No Surrender
Bobby Jean
I'm Goin' Down
Glory Days
Dancing in the Dark
My Hometown

1986

LIVE/1975–85

Thunder Road
Adam Raised a Cain
Spirit in the Night
4th of July, Asbury Park (Sandy)
Paradise by the "C"
Fire
Growin' Up
It's Hard to Be a Saint in the City
Backstreets
Rosalita (Come Out Tonight)
Raise Your Hand
Hungry Heart
Two Hearts
Cadillac Ranch
You Can Look (But You Better Not Touch)

Independence Day
Badlands
Because the Night
Candy's Room
Darkness on the Edge of Town
Racing in the Street
This Land Is Your Land
Nebraska
Johnny 99
Reason to Believe
Born in the U.S.A.
Seeds
The River
War
Darlington Count
Working on the Highway
The Promised Land
Cover Me
I'm on Fire
Bobby Jean

My Hometown
Born to Run
No Surrender
Tenth Avenue Freeze-Out
Jersey Girl

1987

TUNNEL OF LOVE

Ain't Got You
Tougher Than the Rest
All That Heaven Will Allow
Spare Parts
Cautious Man
Walk Like a Man
Tunnel of Love
Two Faces
Brilliant Disguise
One Step Up
When You're Alone
Valentine's Day

1992
HUMAN TOUCH

Human Touch

Soul Driver

57 Channels (And Nothin' On)

Cross My Heart

Gloria's Eyes

With Every Wish

Roll of the Dice

Real World

All or Nothin' at All

Man's Job

I Wish I Were Blind

The Long Goodbye

Real Man

Pony Boy

1992
LUCKY TOWN

Better Days

Lucky Town

Local Hero

If I Should Fall Behind

Leap of Faith

The Big Muddy

Living Proof

Book of Dreams

Souls of the Departed

My Beautiful Reward

1993
IN CONCERT/MTV PLUGGED

Red Headed Woman

Better Days

Atlantic City

Darkness on the Edge of Town

Man's Job

Human Touch

Lucky Town

I Wish I Were Blind

Thunder Road

Light of Day

If I Should Fall Behind

Living Proof

My Beautiful Reward

1995
THE GHOST OF TOM JOAD

The Ghost of Tom Joad

Straight Time

Highway 29

Youngstown

Sinaloa Cowboys

The Line

Balboa Park

Dry Lightning

The New Timer

Across the Border

Galveston Bay

*My Best Was Never
Good Enough*

2001

LIVE IN NEW YORK CITY

My Love Will Not Let You Down
Prove It All Night
Two Hearts
Atlantic City
Mansion on the Hill
The River
Youngstown
Murder Incorporated
Badlands
Out in the Street
Tenth Avenue Freeze-Out
Born to Run
Land of Hope and Dreams
American Skin (41 Shots)

2002

THE RISING

Lonesome Day
Into the Fire
Waitin' on a Sunny Day
Nothing Man
Countin' on a Miracle
Empty Sky
Worlds Apart
Let's Be Friends (Skin to Skin)
Further On (Up the Road)
The Fuse
Mary's Place
You're Missing
The Rising
Paradise
My City of Ruins

2005

DEVILS & DUST

Devils & Dust
All the Way Home
Reno
Long Time Comin'
Black Cowboys

Maria's Bed
Silver Palomino
Jesus Was an Only Son
Leah
The Hitter
All I'm Thinkin' About
Matamoros Banks

2006

HAMMERSMITH ODEON LONDON '75

Thunder Road
Tenth Avenue Freeze-Out
Spirit in the Night
Lost In The Flood
Mona/She's the One
Born to Run
The E Street Shuffle/Havin' A Party
It's Hard to Be a Saint in the City
Backstreets
Kitty's Back
Jungleland
Rosalita (Come Out Tonight)
4th of July, Asbury Park (Sandy)
Detroit Medley
For You
Quarter to Three/Closing Credits

2006

WE SHALL OVERCOME: THE SEEGER SESSIONS

Old Dan Tucker
Jesse James
Mrs. McGrath
O Mary Don't You Weep
John Henry
Erie Canal
Jacob's Ladder
My Oklahoma Home
Eyes on the Prize
Shenandoah
Pay Me My Money Down

We Shall Overcome
Froggie Went a Courtin'
Buffalo Gals (bonus track)
How Can I Keep from Singing? (bonus track)
How Can a Poor Man Stand Such Times and Live? (bonus track)
Bring 'Em Home (bonus track)
American Land (bonus track)

2007

LIVE IN DUBLIN

Atlantic City
Old Dan Tucker
Eyes on the Prize
Jesse James
Further On (Up The Road)
O Mary Don't You Weep
Erie Canal
If I Should Fall Behind
My Oklahoma Home
Highway Patrolman
Mrs. McGrath
How Can a Poor Man Stand Such Times and Live?
Jacob's Ladder
Long Time Comin'
Open All Night
Pay Me My Money Down
Growin' Up
When the Saints Go Marching In
This Little Light of Mine
American Land
Blinded By the Light
Love of the Common People (bonus track)
We Shall Overcome (bonus track)

2007

MAGIC

Radio Nowhere
You'll Be Comin' Down
Livin' in the Future

Your Own Worst Enemy
Gypsy Biker
Girls in Their Summer Clothes
I'll Work for Your Love
Magic
Last to Die
Long Walk Home
Devil's Arcade
Terry's Song

2009

WORKING ON A DREAM

Outlaw Pete
My Lucky Day
Working on a Dream
Queen of the Supermarket
What Love Can Do
This Life
Good Eye
Tomorrow Never Knows
Life Itself
Kingdom of Days
Surprise, Surprise
The Last Carnival
The Wrestler (bonus track)

SINGLES

1973	Blinded by the Light	1980	Hungry Heart	1984	Dancing in the Dark
1973	Spirit in the Night	1981	Fade Away	1984	Cover Me
1975	Born to Run	1981	Sherry Darling	1984	Born in the U.S.A.
1976	Tenth Avenue Freeze-Out	1981	The River	1985	I'm on Fire
1978	Prove It All Night	1981	Cadillac Ranch	1985	Glory Days
1978	Badlands	1982	Atlantic City	1985	I'm Goin' Down
1978	The Promised Land	1982	Open All Night	1985	My Hometown

1985	Santa Claus Is Comin' to Town
1986	War
1987	Fire
1987	Born to Run (live)
1987	Brilliant Disguise
1987	Tunnel of Love
1988	One Step Up
1988	Tougher Than the Rest
1988	Spare Parts
1992	Human Touch
1992	57 Channels (And Nothin' On)
1992	Better Days
1992	Leap of Faith
1993	Lucky Town
1994	Streets of Philadelphia
1995	Murder Incorporated
1995	Hungry Heart (reissue)
1995	The Ghost of Tom Joad
1995	Secret Garden

1998	Sad Eyes
2002	The Rising
2002	Lonesome Day
2003	Waitin' on a Sunny Day
2005	Devils & Dust
2005	All the Way Home
2007	Radio Nowhere
2008	Girls in Their Summer Clothes
2008	Working on a Dream
2008	My Lucky Day
2008	The Wrestler